CLOCK WORM

by Charlie

Clockworm

Foreword

Charlie is a writer. A writer who has at times struggled to find her voice. This anthology of poems written over the course of 7 years serve as a reminder to the power of perseverance in an increasingly immediate world.

We often forget life's incredible teachings but these poems bring us straight back to reality with hard hitting truths. I, myself, have found comfort and solace in her reviews of ice cream lollies and her attitude towards death. Bantah.

Charlie is someone who also exhibits an extraordinary gift for retaining information. Where else would you find someone who has knowledge of both horse insurance as well as what Jesus wore?

No honestly, where else would you find someone like that? I have got a horse in my stables who has started genuflecting and I'm worried he's gonna put his knee out.

Anyway.

Enjoy.

Max Fosh

Charlie

Train

Marks train gets in at 10
Does he get into kings cross?
I can meet him
he will be there
I'm going to wear hair jewellery

A Fab Lolly

You look just like a lolly
a mini milk
underrated ice lolly
Fab
They are the worst!!! Burn them!!!

Life's Questions

What can I bring?

The Xoxo's

haha xoxo
Sounds good! Xoxo
Hope you're well xoxo
Shall I come to yours? Xoxo

The Xoxo's Reprise

she'll be a bit star struck xoxo
What driving snacks do you prefer? Xoxo
It is going to be magic xoxo

Covid

I thought I had Covid on Monday night
but it turns out I was just hot.

Life Questions
7? 730? 8?

Life Questions
Do we need to rsvp?

Death

My mum is gonna die when she meets you
Please also only say nice things about me
There will be no ouija or calling of spirits
Haha bantah

25

I've double booked I'm so sorry and can't
people 25 and under go free

Life Questions

You made a gif?!?! How is this done?

Life Questions

Is it going to be like a live version of glee?

Charlie

Life Questions
Does anyone know a private accountant our age?

Life Questions
Is that okay for everyone?

Boyfriend

I may have accidentally got a new boyfriend
I'm very very up for this

Life Questions

Am I the queen of balance and aesthetics?

Charlie

Accountants

I think accountants going extinct
Very awkward going back
downstairs to my parents

Life Questions

Just wondering if you still
wanna use my cheer outfit?

Life Questions
Something that will soak up booze?

Life Questions
Need any honey?

Life Questions

Dress up?

Drunk

I am awake but think I might still be drunk
Well this turned out well

Life Questions

what about the fact that pregnancies are 10 months instead of 9?

Single

A catch like that won't be single for long. Please come and share your power

Jesus

Jesus is leading the resurrection in a suit of armour and a cowboy hat.
Is there a theme? A dress code? An arrival time?
Oh Jesus

Life Questions

Would anyone be up for starting
a very low key writing group?

Gurl

Oooooooooh gurl
Sounds good to me

Drama

Got drama
How DARE YOU attack us in this way?
I will be updating daily

Charlie

Life Questions

Is there a theme?
A dress code?
An arrival time?

Diseased

I am currently diseased
Especially if that something is maybe pizza shaped
V pumped for this

Pumped

Ugh two lmaos my bad
Um....YEAH
V pumped for this

Life Questions

do people's washing machines really
make that many different sounds?

Charlie

Terrible

Okay this was hard and I'm terrible
I can safely say horse insurance
is probably off the market

Life Questions

I didn't want to be too early lol
but will that be too late?

Twirl

lets just start doing meth
plus then we can pretend
we are florence and twril around

Best

I cannot wait for this
Don't mess with the best
because the best don't mess

Charlie

Armour

Jesus is leading the resurrection
in a suit of armour and a cowboy hat guys

Font

they've nicked your bloody font

Clockworm

Merch

Give us BAROQUE
roundabout merch

Haha

Paaaha
hahaha

Charlie

Brunch

Will and Lucy
 are coming for brunch
on Sunday
1130/12

The best evening

Gonna
have
the BEST EVENING

Clockworm

Girls

OMG
MAX
THESE
GIRLS
WERE
IN
MY
YEAR
AT
SCHOOL
HAHAHAHAHAHAHA

Printed in Great Britain
by Amazon